SNATCHED FROM HELL

So Little Is Known

A real-life testimony of one man's death experience and finding truth in the light of Jesus.

ROBERT McNAMARA

Copyright © 2017 Aileen McNamara

Snatched From Hell: So Little is Known
By Robert McNamara

All rights reserved. No part of this book may be used or reproduced by any means, graphic, electronic, or mechanical, including photocopying, recording, taping or by any information storage retrieval system without the written permission of the publisher except in the case of brief quotations embodied in critical articles and reviews. Because of the dynamic nature of the Internet, any web addresses or links contained in this book may have changed since publication and may no longer be valid. The views expressed in this work are solely those of the author and do not necessarily reflect the views of the publisher, and the publisher hereby disclaims any responsibility for them.

ISBN- 13: 978-1546626077
ISBN- 10: 1546626077

All Scripture quotations, unless otherwise indicated, are taken from the King James Version of the Holy Bible. All Scripture quotations are used by permission.

Scripture quotations marked (NIV) are taken from the Holy Bible, New International Version®, NIV®. Copyright © 1973, 1978, 1984, 2011 by Biblica, Inc.™ Used by permission of Zondervan. All rights reserved worldwide. www.zondervan.com. The "NIV" and "New International Version" are trademarks registered in the United States Patent and Trademark Office by Biblica, Inc.™

Publishing Assistance/Editing/Interior Book Design/Cover Creation:
CBM Christian Book Editing
www.christian-book-editing.com

Printed in the United States of America

DEDICATION

Lovingly dedicated to my Grandmother, Mother Jerry, and to my wife, Aileen.

"I give them eternal life, and they shall never perish; no one will snatch them from out of my hand." (John 10:28 NIV)

May God reveal Himself to you and lead you to everlasting life!

INTRODUCTION

Brenda Smith

Snatched from Hell: So Little Is known is the remarkable true-life story of Robert McNamara, leading up to his incredible death experience after falling dead from a heart attack for an unknown amount of time before the paramedics arrived. Prior to Robert's heart attack, he thought believing in "spiritual stuff" was, as he called it, "baloney".

His experience and testimony has been put in this powerful book, so that others might know and believe upon the Lord Jesus Christ and to understand that Heaven and hell really exist.

When I first heard of this incredible story, I remembered being completely intrigued. I felt so compelled to find out more about this story that I quickly found his wife, Aileen, who is a member of our church. I introduced myself and wouldn't you know it, she had a copy of the DVD of Robert's testimony, "Snatched from Hell" in her car.

I did not get a chance to watch it that Sunday evening, but I had an amazing dream that same night, which prompted me to watch the DVD the next morning.

In the dream I found myself walking from a place of shadow into pure light. I was in a beautiful mansion with huge floral arrangements and marble floors. I looked up and saw a huge staircase. At the base of the royal staircase were two huge and very beautiful flower arrangements.

Immediately, I saw Robert McNamara. I saw the back of his white hair first, then he turned around and I saw his big blue, piercing eyes. He smiled at me with such joy. And I thought, *"That's . . . that guy! The guy who died and came back to life, Robert McNamara."* (I had met Robert McNamara previously at our church and seen him on a regular basis. Since then, he recently has passed on into glory in 2016.)

Suddenly, he was standing right in front of me. I was surprised at first because he was by the stairs, arranging flowers. (At that time, I knew what he did in Heaven because I thought, *Oh, he makes the beautiful arrangements in Heaven.*)

Now "in the blink of an eye," he was standing closer to me, full of joy, and younger, but still with white hair. He looked perfectly healthy. I said, "You're Robert, and you make beautiful flower arrangements in Heaven."

He nodded his head, smiling.

He said, "We are going to make some beautiful arrangements together."

In the next scene, he was holding twelve golden rods. They

were long rods, tall and gleaming, and pure gold. He chose one and pulled the long golden rod from the bundle of golden rods he was holding, that were arranged like a bouquet of flowers, and said, "I have given you the authority."

He said, "Beautiful arrangements will be made. Others must know."

I took the golden rod, felt overjoyed and the dream ended.

With this dream still in my mind and heart, it is with great joy that I present to you this book. I must tell you that this book, and the subject of "salvation" is very dear to God's heart. Choosing God's salvation is the most important decision one will ever make in their life. The Bible mentions that, "I tell you, now is the time of God's favor, now is the day of salvation," (2 Corinthians 6:2). In short, we are never guaranteed our "tomorrows", and today is the time, now is the day to choose salvation. The Bible also states that it is not the will of the Father that any should perish. (John 3:16 NIV)

I believe additionally that this book has an important message to anyone that questions life beyond death. Our physical bodies only house a spirit, one that is eternal. As Robert learned, there is a Heaven, and there is a hell. If you have not accepted Jesus Christ as your personal Lord and Savior, follow this man's testimony, as one who did not believe in God at all. In fact, he was an atheist, and believed that all who went to church were incredibly "weak" to believe in God.

After dying from a heart attack one day while jogging along the California coast, and experiencing hell, demons, and the complete and utter terror, that included a terrible darkness and separation from any kind of life, to include God - Robert McNamara's book will change your point of view on Heaven, hell, the Bible, salvation and God's Word.

You will see throughout this book that God had His hand upon Robert's life from the beginning – all thanks to his praying Grandmother, Mother Jerry. You will also see that God saved Robert several times from death, in addition to divine appointments along the way.

Looking back upon your life, you might also see the mighty hand of God at work in your life as well. And if you have a loved one praying for you, never doubt that God is listening!

SNATCHED FROM HELL

So Little Is Known

A real-life testimony of one man's death experience and finding truth in the light of Jesus.

ROBERT McNAMARA

TABLE OF CONTENTS

Introduction v

Chapter One
The Beginning 13

Chapter Two
Starting Over 23

Chapter Three
War Again? 35

Chapter Four
Transitions 43

Chapter Five
Wedding Bells 55

Chapter Six
A Strange Occurrence 65

Chapter Seven
Life was Good 69

Chapter Eight
In the Blink of an Eye – Life Changed 73

Chapter Nine
Where's Dad? 79

Chapter Ten
Changes in Me 89

Chapter Eleven
Home Again 93

Chapter Twelve
What Do I Have to Do? 101

Conclusion 113

Invitation to Christ 114

Salvation Prayer 115

Aileen McNamara's Testimony 117

About the Author 119

CHAPTER ONE

The Beginning

When the train pulled into Los Angeles, Jerry took a piece of paper from her purse and glanced at it. She was supposed to take the Red Car to Long Beach. She asked and was told that it was right around the second corner. She liked the little red electric train as it made its way out of Los Angeles, stopping from time to time, but finally ending up in downtown Long Beach. Bob, my dad, was there to pick her up. He smiled, took her bag, and then shook her hand. (They didn't know each other well enough to hug.) *He's a handsome man*, Jerry thought, with his wavy brown hair and a smile that looked like it came right out of Ireland.

"How's the baby doing?" Jerry asked, as she smiled back at him.

"Not too well," Bob replied. "He has some sort of sickness. We had a doctor come over who said that he had the flu."

Jerry glanced over at him, but he had already started walking toward the car. Now the uneasiness within her became stronger.

Neither one of them was good at small talk. The ride was quiet as Jerry looked at the open fields and listened to the motor of the Model A, as they made their way to a little town called Wilmington.

My father and mother had rented a nice little home with two bedrooms. As Jerry went through the living room, she saw the standup piano. Fay had learned to play in the Convent, and she heard that Bob had a wonderful tenor voice. He led the way to the back bedroom. As soon as Jerry entered, Fay went right into her arms. They hugged for an unusually long time, but Jerry could see the crib over her daughter's shoulder. She broke the hug and went to the crib. She looked down at me. I was crying. She touched my face and then put her hands on my tummy. Immediately Jerry sensed something was terribly wrong, and it seemed to be more serious than the flu.

"Has he been throwing up?"

"Yes, everyday," Fay answered, "sometimes two or three

times a day. And Mama, he cries all the time, even in his sleep."

"This child has to go to the hospital right now," Jerry said as calmly as possible.

"The doctor said it was the flu," Fay answered.

"The doctor was wrong." Without another word Jerry picked me up, wrapped a blanket around me and handed me to my mother. My father had already left the room, and Jerry heard the front door opening. The car was already running as we left the house. Jerry sat in the back seat as they drove to the San Pedro hospital. No one spoke, but I was whimpering.

The doctor wasn't with me very long before he went out to the waiting room. " Has the baby passed any feces since he was born?" he asked my mother.

Fear came over her face. "No. He's only peed."

"What about vomiting? Has he done much of that?"

"Yes," Fay answered, "that's why we called the doctor and he came to our house. He said Bobby had the flu."

"He has a complete obstruction within his intestines. It's necessary for him to have immediate surgery."

Fay looked at Bob and then at her mother. Both nodded in agreement. "All right," she answered. Now the tears were welling up. "I don't know why I didn't think about that. I just don't know why!" She was crying now.

The doctor bent down to her ear and said softly, "We'll take care of him. We'll do it right now." Standing upright, he looked at Bob, then turned and walked quickly down the hallway. My dad came and sat next to my mom, putting his arm around her.

Jerry closed her eyes for a moment and said a silent, very direct prayer to God. "Save my grandson, my only grandson." She wished that she could scream it out, but silently she kept saying the prayer over and over again.

She would not stop knocking. She started to have thoughts about her dead son, but her mind said, "No!" She would only think about God and Bobby. She knew that Jesus was always there ready to be called on. Once again, she said the prayer as she moved to the other side of her daughter and took her hand. She couldn't stop, and she didn't.

They waited two hours, and then the doctor came down the hallway. All three got up and walked toward him.

"He had a loop of bowel in a hernial ring. We straightened it, and his bowels will be fine now. We'll keep him a few days for observation, but everything looks very positive."

Fay stood before him with tears in her eyes, starting to reach out her hand to take his, brought it back, then reached out again. The doctor took it and smiled as he patted the tearful woman's hand.

"What would have happened if we hadn't brought him in?" Bob asked. Fay had already turned to him, and he was holding her.

The doctor paused for a moment, and then said straightforwardly, "He would have died from peritonitis." He paused again, then added, "To tell you the truth, we don't know how he lasted as long as he did." He patted Fay's shoulder and turned back toward the hallway. Then he said over his shoulder, "You can stay with him as long as you want, whenever you want. He needs someone by him. You can't pick him up, but you can keep touching him."

"Thank God for a good doctor," Jerry murmured. Bob took Jerry's hand as they sat down. Fay went down the hall to be with me.

"I don't know how to thank you. Without you. . ." Bob couldn't finish the sentence. Mother Jerry put her other hand over his.

* * * *

A month had passed when David McNamara, my grandfather, called our home. He was a customs agent in San Pedro.

"How's the boy feelin'?" he asked in his heavy County Cork brogue. Even though he and Grandma Elizabeth just lived a few miles away, it was expected that Bob and his family would come to visit them, as it was done in the old country.

"He's a lot better. He's gaining weight, and his color is really good."

"Glad ta' hear it. When do ya' think he'll be ready for baptism?"

Well, here it was. Bob knew that he would have to face it, but he had hoped it would be much later. There was only one way to do this with his father, direct and to the point. " He's not going to be baptized. Fay made me promise before we married. She wants him to make his own decision about what religion he follows."

"Then why the hell did ya' marry her?"

"Because I love her."

"Didn't I warn ya' about marryin' a Protestant? And what about the child's soul? Do ya' care about that? Ya' gotta remember that the Protestants don't know what the hell their doin'!"

"Why don't I come over, dad, and we can have a couple of drinks together. We can talk more about it." Bob knew that his dad wasn't about to change his mind, but drinking was something that they did well together. He heard a deep sigh before his dad agreed.

My dad kissed my mom goodbye. He wasn't sure if she heard the phone conversation or not. She always seemed to have a sad expression on her face when he was going to his parent's house. She didn't drink, and he knew that she didn't like him doing it either. He had been trying to cut down on it since the birth of his son, but had little success.

Some four or five months later, sometime around Christmas, Bob was notified that he had been excommunicated from the Catholic Church. His father and mother cried, while Bob seemed to take it in stride, talking little about it, yet in his gut, in that deep area, he was angry. He stayed that way.

I found out when I was little that my father had two jobs. First, he told me, was the refinery (I had no idea what that was.) in Wilmington, California. He use to tell me that my Mommy was the prettiest secretary the refinery had ever hired. It was 1934 and "times were hard," I used to hear, and sometimes my Mommy would worry about Daddy being gone too long over at grandpa's house. The second job his other love, he used to call it, was singing. He sang in different places where people went to clubs like the Elks or with somebody called the Masons.

He sang anywhere he could. Every cent he made in overtime he used to pay his singing coach, the same man who trained Nelson Eddie. (He played in movies.) In the mornings, before work, Daddy would sing as he was shaving. Mommy would be in the living room playing the piano. I would be on the toilet laughing, because his voice was so powerful that it would make the toilet seat vibrate slightly, just enough to tickle my fanny. My daddy seemed happy when he sang. I liked being there, being happy with him.

When I was seven, my dad got a chance to perform on the Major Bowes Amateur Hour in New York City, one of the best shows on radio. He stayed with my Aunt Violet and her husband Kenneth in New Jersey. The night Dad performed, Mom, Mother Jerry (what I called my grandma then) and a group of friends from the refinery gathered around the radio. What an exciting time we had. Dad won first place, which meant that he got to go back the next week. He called Mom that night and told her all about it and how good it felt to win. When Mom hung up she started to cry, and Mother Jerry held her. I didn't understand, but when Mother smiled at me I knew everything was all right.

The next week Dad won again, and then the week after that, he won again! This was the first time anybody had won three weeks in a row on the Bowes Show. Mom told me that he had become a celebrity! I didn't know what it meant, but it made me happy, just as happy as my mother and grandmother. When Dad got home, he received a letter from the Metropolitan Opera in New York inviting him to come back at the beginning of the next year for an audition. Wow!

It might have been shortly before Christmas when dad started to feel weak, and pretty soon he became worried about it. Mom finally talked him into seeing a doctor. From there, he went directly to the hospital where I was born in San Pedro. They did some tests on him and found out that he had leukemia. I came to visit my dad in the hospital a couple of times, but then one day my mom told me that my father had died, after being in the hospital for only two weeks.

I'm not sure why, but I wasn't allowed to go to his funeral. Maybe they felt that I was too young, but I'm really not sure. After my dad's death, Mom and I never saw my dad's parents again. As far as I knew, they just seemed to disappear, as if they just moved away. My mom never talked about them, and it took about a year before I didn't think about them anymore.

[How this affected me I didn't know. You are what you are, and I had no idea how I could change it.]

CHAPTER TWO

Starting Over

We moved out of the house in Wilmington and into an upstairs apartment in Long Beach. Mother Jerry lived close by and worked at the local hospital. One day, when I was eight, I fell down the outside stairs. I fell hard, and it hurt a lot, enough that I talked to my mother about it. She called Mother Jerry, and my grandmother hurried over. She checked me over, pressed just below my ribs, and it hurt so much that I cried out. She and Mom took me to the hospital.

On the way or in the hospital, my appendix ruptured. I remember asking the man who was wheeling me down to the operating room, "Am I going to die?" He never answered me, but a man in a white coat walking along side told me that I wasn't going to die. I don't remember whether I believed him or not.

World War II

It was after the war started with Japan, that Mother Jerry married again. There's really not any connection between the two, except that I was eleven and everybody was afraid that the Japanese were going to either bomb California or land on its shores. I remember everyone being nervous about it at the wedding. She married a big Swedish guy named Art who was a fisherman and had a boat down in San Pedro Harbor. Not too long after the marriage, he sold the boat, and they bought a house in Bellflower. When they moved, my Mom had to find another way for somebody to watch after me. She decided on St. Catherine's Military Academy. It was years later that I connected reasons for such a move; Mother Jerry did the same thing with my Mom and her sister when they were young. And as did Mother Jerry, my Mom also made it clear to the Mother Superior that she was not a Catholic, and that she didn't want me proselytized either.

I spent two years in the school. What I remember most about it was that I felt alone. The priest and the sisters who ran the school and the dormitories didn't seem to care about us, accept to get us through the day. I got so I felt the same way about them. All I wanted to do was to stay away from them. We also had a Colonel who retired out of the Army and headed up the military training of all of us. He was scary.

There was some sexual stuff that went on there too. Since there weren't girls around, I'll leave the rest to your imagination.

A year and a half went by. It was in 1944, when my mom told me she was going to get married again. Harvey was a research chemist at the refinery, and I guess they had been going out together when I was in the military school. He was ten years younger than my Mom, but she didn't care. I didn't either. Harvey and I didn't talk much to each other; there didn't seem to be anything to say.

I left the military school when they bought a house in North Long Beach. Our street ran right behind the Sunnyside Mausoleum where my father was interned. Each day when I walked out the front door, I could see the fancy, high, wrought iron fence that ran around the huge place.

On the way to school, I watched the Mausoleum leave my sight. I kept asking myself questions about what it was like in there. I found I was spending so much time thinking about this place and being mad because they had my dad, not me.

In time I decided to go in there and see if I could find where he was. I slowly approached the doors. When I walked in, there was a long marble hall. I saw a lady secretary. She came to me and asked what brought me there.

"My father is buried in this building, but I don't know where."

"Was he cremated or in a crypt?" she asked as she went behind her desk.

"A crypt," I answered, hoping that that was the same thing as a coffin. Behind her, the lady had a long shelf filled with large files and many other folders. "What's your father's name?"

"Robert McNamara," I told her. "And what year did he die?"

"Nineteen thirty-seven." As I said it, she removed one of the large books and placed it on her desk. She found the page she wanted. And then ran her finger down the page. " Yes, here he is. He's in the new wing." I waited. "Would you like me to show you where he is?"

"Yes, please." I answered. She wrote something on a small piece of paper, got up, smiled at me and headed for the door. We walked down another long-marbled hall that looked the same to me as the one I had been in earlier. But then, we made a turn and went down a stairway. There were some lights on, but it wasn't as bright as upstairs. Right in the middle of this lower hallway, some ways down in front of me, nothing was finished. There were scaffolds and containers for holding cement along the bare walls, and a strand of stringed lights hanging from the ceiling. But just before the marbled floor ended, the lady turned to the right into a small, square area that was finished. On one side of the space were sixteen marbled covered crypts. The lady looked down at the paper in her hand and then pointed down to the second level, three rows from the door.

"That's where your father's body is," she said softly, watching my face.

"There's no name," I said, looking at the empty square piece of marble.

"No. That's for the family to take care of," she said softly.

I didn't know what to say. The lady was silent for a

moment, then said, "Would you like to stay for a while?"

"Is that okay?"

"Yes. Just come by and tell me when you're leaving."

"All right." I said as she left. I moved to the opening to the hallway and watched until she turned and went up the stairs. I turned back and stood in front of my father's marble square. The squares around my father all had names on them, but no vases for flowers. I reached out and touched the marble. It was cold and smooth. It had been six years since my father's death. There was very little I remembered about him. I thought I should remember more, but I didn't. I had some photographs of him holding me when I was real little, like two or three maybe; I would look at them, but it didn't help any.

The more I looked at the cold slab, the sadder I got. "When I get the money, I'm going to put his name on here!" I said as I jabbed at the marble. "Right here and big, not small!" I felt my stomach growing tight. I couldn't help it. I started to cry. I put my face against the cold marble and cried some more. I just wish that he was still here, and I could know him.

* * * *

I couldn't seem to stay out of trouble. I stole money from my Mom's purse, stole cigarettes from my aunt and ditched school a few times. I even took Harvey's car out for a spin once, even though I didn't know how to drive. I'd watched Harvey and Mom drive and picked up a little from them. It was fun, but I got beat for it. Every once in a while, my mom would tell me to get down on my hands and knees in the living room, and Harvey would hit me with a razor strap a few times. It hurt pretty good; I'd cry a little, but I really didn't give a damn.

My mom took me to a psychiatrist once, and he gave me some tests. One was an I.Q. test, and I decided that on every question I would put just the opposite from what I thought might be the real answer. A week or so later, Mom told me that my I.Q. was a hundred and six. Thinking that I wasn't very smart, she treated me a little differently after that.

When the Second World War was over, Shell Oil offered a job to Harvey over in Holland, to help rebuild the chemical lab at the refinery that had been demolished by the Nazi's. Harvey and Mom decided that I wasn't going with them, so they sent me to the Chino's Republic for Boys. I was six foot three when I was fifteen and really skinny. I enjoyed sports and played a lot of baseball and basketball.

Steve McQueen and I were roomies. Big deal. He was a pain-in-the-butt, and so was I. So, it was okay because we didn't talk to each other. He didn't give a damn about people, and neither did I.

(Years later, Robert would be contacted by Marshall Terrill who was putting together a book on Steve McQueen's life. If you would like to read about Robert's time being roommates with Steve McQueen, which is a brief one-page documentation, you can read, "Roommates for Life" by Robert McNamara that was published in the book titled, *Steve McQueen, A Tribute to the King of Cool* by Marshall Terrill that includes a forward by Barbara McQueen. Incidentally, years later Robert worked for Dalton Books, and had the pleasure to meet Barbara McQueen and receive a signed copy of the book.)

At the Boy's Republic, they had me cleaning up cow manure in the milk barn until I got good enough in sports. Then they had me taking care of the baseball field. In my second year there, four of us ran away and went back into Long Beach. We walked through Carbon Canyon all night and most of the next day until we ended up in Long Beach. That night, I suggested to the other guys that we sleep at the high school where there was a large grassy area with trees and a lot of bushes, enough to hide in, at least I thought it was enough. I suddenly felt a hand grab me and lift me to my feet. It was a policeman, and another one standing next to him. I looked around for the other guys, but I was the only one there. Without a word, they put me in their car and drove me to the police station. They put me in a little room with a small table and three chairs. I waited alone for about fifteen minutes, and then two large men in suits came in and sat across from me.

"Where were you last night at about midnight?"

"I was asleep at the school, where I was this morning."

"What about the grocery store?"

"What grocery store?" I asked.

There was a long pause as they looked at me, and I looked at them. One of the men got to his feet, stared down at me for a moment, then left the room. I was getting nervous, wondering what was going on. Then the door opened and Joe, a captain in the Army and my Aunt Violet's boyfriend (She had divorced Kenneth years before because he was a drunk.) came into the room with the policeman. He smiled at me, then the officer with me, said, "You go with him. He's taking you back to the school." I wondered how they knew about the school. On the way back to Chino, Joe told me that the police caught the other three guys as they were leaving a closed grocery store, which they had just robbed for food.

I'd heard about the Republics' two-foot long paddle with the holes drilled through it, but never had seen it. I did when I got back to the school. Mr. Graves, the head guy, had me lean over a big oak table with my hands gripping the edge of it. The first shot was so hard that my legs gave out and I flopped over the table. I'd never felt pain like that before. I found out that Harvey's razor strap was a cakewalk. Graves waited until I got back up, then he gave me nine more. For about a week, I couldn't sit, and my butt looked like a red-hot waffle iron.

I was there for three years. When my Mom and Harvey got back from Europe, a move took place to Northern California. Harvey asked for a transfer up to the Martinez refinery, because his family owned a walnut ranch in Contra Costa County. There was an old house in the back of the six-hundred-acre ranch, along with a large barn filled with hay and a corral attached. There were cattle in the back hills and three horses in the corral. This time, they took me with them. I started my senior year of high school in Danville, California. Our old walnut ranch house was about three and a half miles from the school. At first, I walked it, but then I found out that the school had a corral at the back of it. Students were allowed to ride horses there. One of the horses Harvey's family owned was an old paint by the name of Pat. I learned how to ride him. I rode him down the dirt road, then next to the railroad tracks, which led right into town. Pat was pretty docile and good-natured. I rode bareback, and I liked riding him.

The school didn't have many students, maybe a hundred or so. Even though I spent a little time in Junior High in Long Beach where there were girls, I never talked to any of them. I liked a beautiful, dark-haired, quiet girl by the name of Jessie Saunders, even though I never spoke to her. But I did put her name up on my bedroom wall on a piece of wide white tape, and then printed her name with some kind of paint that glowed in the dark. I guess you could call her my first girlfriend, but it certainly was one-sided. But now, I was seventeen and hoped that things would be different. Harvey let me work on the ranch, and I made enough money to put down on a used 41 Ford coupe. Every month I paid Harvey a little bit until I owned it.

I was more fascinated with girls than I was in with classes. They were so new and looked so much better than I really thought possible. But I still didn't know how to talk to them, and there were so many pretty ones! So, the first thing I did was to pretend I knew what I was doing. Some of the girls looked at me and smiled, even before I knew them, so I finally figured out, the first thing to do was smile back! But then what? Do you just go up and start talking? Most of the kids in the school had grown up around each other, and everybody knew everybody, which made it a little weird finding friends. But there were a few guys that didn't seem to hang out with anyone else, so I was drawn to them. After all these years, we're still friends and contact each other from time to time.

In that year, I had sex with a girl. My friends told me she was "easy", and she was. On the way home from the movies she moved close to me in my car and put her hand on my thigh. When we got to the front of her house she asked me to move from behind the steering wheel. We kissed a few times, then she unzipped me, then putting her leg over me she sat on top of me. It was over quickly. I took her to her door, and on the way back to my car, I knew something had been missing even though it felt good. After that, whenever I saw her at school, she never even looked at me.

CHAPTER THREE

War Again?

The Korean War came in 1950, and four of us, who graduated high school together, joined the U.S. Navy, thinking it was safer than the Army. During the four years, none of us saw each other again, but we all lived through it. One thing I would like to talk about, even though, at the time, it seemed incidental.

I received a letter from my Grandmother on my Father's side. My Father's dad had died some years before. She moved to Oregon; and she wanted to hear from me. She printed out her address in Pendleton and her phone number too. As soon as I read it, I threw it away. How she had got the letter to me, I didn't find out until years later, after she died. Somehow, she had found my mother's address, wrote to her, and my mom had sent her my ship's name and all the necessary info.

Another incident that in later years I thought a lot about happened early one morning; I was asleep in my bunk back aft when the battle station alarm went off. I'd heard it before, but only for drills. We were in the Sea of Japan off the coast of North Korea, so I knew this wasn't a drill. I got out of my bunk as quickly as possible, as did all the rest down there, dressed, and ran to my station, which was up forward in the radar room. I'd been at my station a minute or so, when the radar man next to me told me that we were going into Wonsan Harbor, running point for the heavy cruiser Los Angeles. I was there about fifteen minutes when I felt a shudder that seemed to go through the entire ship. Everybody in radar looked at each other. The word came down quickly from the bridge. We'd been hit back aft by canon fire from the Korean guns along the coast. Later we learned that the U.S. Los Angeles retaliated and blew up the guns that were firing at us. Without losing speed, we turned and got out of the harbor.

After general quarters had ended, I went back aft to my bunk. I couldn't believe it. The shell had entered the deck right about my quarters and everything was in ruins. The three-tiered bunks were gone; our footlockers had huge holes in them from shrapnel. The shell had missed the magazine locker, where they kept the five-inch shells for the turret above us, by three or four feet. If they would have hit that magazine locker, our aft including our props, would have blown up, and we'd have sunk immediately. It was winter, and the water was in the high thirties. Maybe you could last five or six minutes in water that cold. I looked in my locker and saw that the heal of one of my dress shoes has a piece of shrapnel in it that looked like a large twisted conch shell, with its bottom pointed like a needle. I kept it for a while, but then thought, *why am I keeping this thing?* I threw it over the side. We went into Japan for repairs and shore leave.

During our few weeks there, I met a Japanese girl. Well, I didn't really just meet her; I paid for her. She was at a Geisha house. We liked each other though and met sometimes outside of the house. One day she told me that she was pregnant, and that the baby was mine. Doing the "work" that she did, I didn't know whether to believe her or not. I never saw her again.

Some fifty or sixty miles north of Wonsan in North Korea there was a short span of railroad line that ran directly along the coast that brought supplies from China down to the battle lines. There might have been three or four thousand feet of open territory before it entered a tunnel and went inland. The only time the supplies were brought down was at nighttime. The destroyer I was on was given orders to stop the supplies. A plan was devised. The destroyer would stay a few thousand yards off the coast, and the captain's gig would be used to go near the shoreline and wait for the sound of the oncoming train. In the captain's gig were four men. A lieutenant, the leader, a boatswain mate to run the gig, a gunner's mate to fire the BAR (Browning automatic rifle), and a radio man to notify the destroyer when they should fire. Even though I was an electronics technician, I got selected to be the radioman. Why, I don't know. We lowered the captain's gig into the water around midnight and made our way toward the shore. We wanted to stay just outside the breakwater. There were no lights at all on the shoreline, and we had no running lights. It was dark out there. The boatswain cut the motor. How he knew when to do it, I don't know, but we could hear the waves breaking not too far in front of us. We used no anchor, but the water seemed very calm. We waited, maybe a half hour or so. Then we heard the sound of a freight train engine. The lieutenant pointed at me to notify the ship. I did. I told them that we heard it, but it is not visible yet. Get ready to fire. Then we heard the brakes of the train. It was slowing down and then the sound of the brakes stopped. It was not visible. The lieutenant looked into the darkness with his binoculars.

"They're in a tunnel. Why the hell did they stop?"

We waited and listened. Then the boatswain's mate said

to the lieutenant, "They're building up steam, sir."

"By God, I think you're right."

Another minute or two passed, when the train came out as fast as it could. As soon as I saw it, I radioed the ship, "Fire! Fire!" And they did. The first two shells were supposed to be flare shells that would light up the entire track area along the beach. We waited. About a half-mile inland the two shells went off. They lit up the far-off hills.

"What the hell are they doing?" shouted the lieutenant.

I didn't pass that along to the ship. We watched as the engine and about twelve cars went across the beach area and into the southern tunnel. We listened as the sounds of the train became fainter and fainter as it moved inland. With a curt command the officer ordered the boatswain to get us back to the ship. I had a feeling that they knew we were out here.

The next night, we tried it again. This time, the captain told the lieutenant to go for the boilers of the engine using the BAR (Browning Automatic Rifle) if the five-inchers from the ship didn't succeed. Once again, the wily engineer stopped in the tunnel and built up steam. This time when he came out, the flare shells from the ship were on line, and the gunner's mate could see the engine and even the driver. He let go, aiming for the boilers. He hit them, and steam started to go everywhere. Koreans were running away from the train. The shells from the five inchers were on the mark. Sand, portions of railroad tracks and some of the cars were being blasted. I don't know why, but during this time, for some reason, I looked over the gunnel (side) of the gig. There was something in the water, maybe six or seven feet from us. It looked like a square framed box filled with some kind of grass. And on the side, I could see, were steel shafts about two feet long. Then I got it; they were detonators. It was a crude looking mine, and it was coming nearer to the gig. It was too far for my arm to reach, so I put one of my long legs over the side, making sure that my foot didn't hit the detonators. My foot landed solidly against the boxed frame of the mine.

"There's a mine," I yelled, over the noise from the BAR. I got no response. I kept my eyes on the mine. "Let's get the hell out of here! It's a mine, damn it! A mine!" The boatswain looked over my shoulder into the water then started the motor. We slowly moved away from the ominous looking thing, making sure the prop didn't draw it closer. We went back to the ship. We didn't go on that mission again. The next morning, we heard that Navy planes came over the track and blew up everything on the beach. We also heard that three days later the

North Koreans and probably the Chinese too, rebuilt the rail line, and the trains were running again. Also, we found out there was a river just north of the tunnel that poured into the Japanese Sea. The Koreans were sending the homemade mines out from there.

CHAPTER FOUR

Transitions

In 1954, I had been out of the Navy for about two weeks and back in my parents' home. Even though it was late in the morning, I was still in bed. Harvey, my stepfather, came into the room, which he never did, because we didn't talk much to each other.

"What are you going to do now?" he asked.

"Right now?"

"No, with your life. What do you want to do?"

"I've got no idea."

"How about college? You can get a monthly amount of money through the government for spending time in the Navy."

"What would I study?" I never thought about going back to school.

"Why don't you go to Contra Costa Junior College for a year? That way you might find out what you want to do."

Since I didn't have anything else to do, it sounded pretty good. "Yeah, maybe I'll do that." Harvey left my room. I had a feeling my mother set this up, but even so, it would give me something to do. So, I went over to the college, enrolled, and started in September.

I took the usual stuff, English, Math, Speech, etc., the classes you had to have if you wanted to go on to a four-year college. Most of the time, I was bored, but I did my homework and knew that if this was all there was going to be, I wouldn't want to spend another three years doing it.

One day at noontime, my Speech teacher, Bess Whitcomb, came into the Student Hall where I was having lunch. She sat down next to me. I'd never seen her in here before, plus she never said two words to me outside of the classroom. I had my mouth full as she looked at me. She was an older lady, near her seventies, and from what I had heard about her, she was an actress in New York, and a pretty well-known one from what people said. I looked back at her.

We're going to do a couple of one act plays here in the Student Hall in a few weeks," she said, never taking her eyes off of me.

"Oh," I said, not knowing what to say.

"One of the plays is named, 'The Man in the Bowler Hat.' she said, watching me eat. What the hell was I supposed to say back to her? I kept quiet. She continued, "It's a farce, with a heroine, hero and villain. It's a lot of fun, and the student body will love it."

"Good," I said as I wiped my mouth. "I'll be sure to come to it."

"I want you to play the villain."

What the hell was going on? I thought. "I've never acted before and don't want to."

Mrs. Whitcomb looked over her glasses at me and said evenly, "Do you want a good grade in Speech?"

I couldn't believe this! I really didn't want to talk to this old broad anymore, and I certainly didn't want to make butt in front of the whole student body. "You know that this smacks of blackmail?"

"Yes, it does," she answered with genuine smile. "Sometimes that's what teachers have to do." She stood up. "Our first reading will be tomorrow at 3PM. You'll be there, won't you?"

I knew the old lady wasn't fooling. She'd probably flunk me if I didn't go. I nodded in the affirmative, and then watched her as she walked out of the building. I had to admit, that in her day, there was little doubt that she was a beauty.

Acting was weird and really foreign. I didn't have any trouble remembering my lines, because there were so few of them. But I certainly felt uncomfortable and out of place during rehearsals. A few days before the performance, Bess Whitcomb, drew me aside and said quietly, "You're missing the point, Bob."

"What do you mean?"

"You seem uncomfortable. Is that right?" "Yes."

"The reason is, you're not being your normal self."

"What do you mean?"

"You don't care much for people, and you're curt and sometimes even rude. Be like that. That fits the man in the bowler hat perfectly."

She was right. So, from then on, I treated everybody as though I didn't care at all what they did or what they said. I just went around trying to get my money. It felt pretty good. For dress rehearsals they put me in black boots with lifts in them and this rather tall bowler hat. I probably stood nearly seven feet tall. The story was simple. A pretty blonde lady with a little baby could not pay her rent, and I owned the place. She and her handsome boyfriend tried to talk me into giving her more time but to no avail. I wanted her out now, and it was in the dead of winter.

We did the play in the round within the Student Body Hall. There were people all around us. When you came on "stage" you had to walk right down an aisle with students on either side of you. When I came down the aisle the audience started booing and stamping their feet, knowing how bad I really was. At first it shocked me, but then I started liking it. It seemed to fit right into who I was.

The next year I majored in Dramatic Literature at San Jose State and had a great time, which continued for three years. When I graduated, I decided to move down to the Hollywood area and see what I could do. Though I had looked forward to it, trying to get work was pretty tough. I went to a couple of acting classes, one with Jeff Corey and another with Brian Hutton. They were both good teachers, and I learned to do things besides being a self-centered grump. I did get a few calls from "Night Court" and played a policeman from time to time. It didn't pay much but it was great fun. I did a couple of very bad movies in Deadwood, South Dakota for the Corman Brothers. The movies were so bad I can't remember their titles and as far as I know they were never shown.

In 1960, a strike took place that covered all the studios and television too. I couldn't find any work. I decided to go back to college and get my Masters. At least, I could teach drama after that. I called Mother Jerry and Art down in Bellflower and asked if I could stay at their place while I went to Long Beach State College. There was a pause on the other end. I wouldn't blame her if she said no.

"Oh. Then come on down. We've got room for you in a

trailer next to the house." I'd forgotten that their house had only two bedrooms, and my grandfather snored so loudly that they used both of them. So, I went and stayed in the trailer. The bed wasn't long enough, but I slept at an angle with my feet hanging in the aisle.

I filled out the necessary papers at the college and asked that my transcript be sent down from San Jose State. I started in September of 1960. An unusual thing happened after I'd been there just a few days. I got called into the office of the head of Drama Department; Dr. David Seivers sat behind the desk. He smiled, introduced himself; we shook hands, and I sat in the chair in front of the desk.

"I got your transcript from San Jose. You did a great deal of work up there." I just smiled and nodded. "You've been an actor in Hollywood for over a year?"

"Yes," I said, "and also a bouncer at a beer joint on Sunset Boulevard."

He laughed and looked down at my transcript. "We're going to be doing the West Coast premiere of Eugene O'Neill's play, 'Moon for the Misbegotten.' Do you know it?"

"I read it in college. Pretty heavy stuff."

"I'd like you to play Tyrone."

"You mean tryout for it?"

"No, play it."

Tyrone is the lead. He is a walking definition of failure. He was fixated on his mother and was a self-destroying alcoholic. Though I'm not an alcoholic, and my mother and I had a rather silent, yet moderate relationship. I certainly could number myself with the failures. I accepted the part.

A couple of days later Seivers had tryouts for the rest of the parts. I stood on stage reading with all the ladies that were trying out for the part of Josie, who is supposed to be grotesquely large in stature, so much so that her father, Phil Hogan, an Irish farmer, feels that this tragedy of nature can only be remedied by marrying off his daughter and then trying to save his farm. So, comes Tyrone, his barfly buddy.

As I stood and read with the ladies trying out for the part, there were none who fit O'Neill's description. Then one young lady came on stage that was so beautiful, I had a difficult time concentrating on the work at hand.

After finishing reading, though she was very adept at it, I knew she would never get the part. She was about five-foot-seven, with a waist I could probably put my hands around. I watched her as she walked off stage and headed for her seat with the other students trying out. She stopped, turned around and looked at me, no smile, just a look. It was enough for me. I found out that her name was Aileen, and she was an art major with a drama minor. I started meandering through the halls of the art department until I ran into her. We talked a while, and I asked her out. She accepted. She was twenty-three, married but separated, wanting a divorce, but her husband said no. It made little difference to me; I wanted to be with her. Something she said on the first date, made me know that we would be seeing each other again.

"Does everybody call you Bob?"

"Everybody except my grandmother; she calls me Bobby." She said, "Would you mind if I called you Robert?"

I'd never been called that before, but it sounded just right coming from her beautiful mouth. I laughed and immediately agreed. Through the next two months our relationship quickly became more and more intimate. One night she even came to visit me at my luxury trailer for a few hours.

It was a strange way to live for me. Every morning I would go into the house to shower and then have breakfast with Mother Jerry and Art. In the evenings, when I had to go to the bathroom, I'd have to go into the house again. I'd come through the back door, through the kitchen, then the small dining room, and I would see Mother Jerry in the living room sitting in her doily-covered rocker with a goose-necked lamp that peered over her shoulder, throwing light on the book in her lap. On her head she wore a green-shaded plastic visor, the kind worn by dealers in gambling halls in the thirty and forties. Most of the time when I'd come through I'd tiptoe, because she would have her eyes closed and she would be mumbling to herself sometimes when reading, she would look up at me, smile and immediately go back to her book. I didn't know what to make of the old lady, but she was amusing to look at with that plastic visor and her mumblings. Art once told me that she did this every night, sometimes for a couple of hours. He said that the book in her lap was a Bible.

Mother Jerry's breakfasts were always great: eggs, bacon, pancakes and sometimes French toast. But the trouble was that Aileen and I were spending more time together, and I was getting less and less sleep. It was getting harder to get out of that little bed and make it to the shower. But after I put on my clothes and left the bathroom, there would be Art and Mother Jerry sitting at the kitchen table waiting for me. I don't know how she did it, but the food was always hot, ready to be eaten. It was one of those mornings when I felt my grandmother's eyes on me. I looked up from my plate, and she was staring at me. "What?"

"Bobby, I know what you're supposed to be."

She really caught me off guard. "What I'm supposed to be?" I glanced at Art, and I saw that he was curious too.

"Yes." She paused. I could see that she was very serious about what she was about to say. "You're supposed to be a preacher."

I couldn't believe what she had just said. I looked at Art, who was just as surprised as I was. We both started laughing. Art knew my character just as well as I did. I no more believed in God or an afterlife than I did the man-in-the-moon. I glanced at Mother Jerry. Her face was solemn, and she stared at me. I stopped laughing. She pointed a gnarled old finger at me, and said, "Bobby, you're going to be surprised at what is going to happen to you. I've prayed for you every day of your life."

I had never seen her so intent or her eyes so penetrating. I didn't know what to say, so I finished my breakfast without speaking. She never said another word about the subject.

CHAPTER FIVE

Wedding Bells

"Moon for the Misbegotten" had finished its run, when Aileen said she had something to tell me. She was pregnant. Before this, just before the first time that we made love together, she had told me that she had been unable to conceive when she was with her husband. He was unwilling to give her a divorce even though they were separated, and she said that she would never go back to him. Now, here she stood, waiting for my answer. This had happened to me before, but this time there was no doubt that I was the father. I didn't know what to say, so without thought, I answered, "What are you going to do about it?" A look of surprise, or maybe dismay, crossed her face. Without another word, she turned and walked away. I watched her go and felt stupid.

A week later, I heard from one of my drama teachers in Hollywood that he was directing a play and that they had a role in it for me. Even though it was a small part, I packed up from my grandmother's trailer, and rented a tiny, one-room apartment in West Los Angeles, across the walkway from a friend of mine from San Jose State. The play, "The Connection," was held in a theater where dinner was served to the audience, and the play was performed as they sat at their tables. It was a unique idea for Hollywood, but one that both the audience and the players enjoyed. It wasn't too many nights into the run when Aileen stood before me. I had just turned around backstage, and there she was.

"I'm going to keep the baby. You know that it's yours. I need to know if you want me to be with you, or do you want me to leave for good?"

The woman was straightforward and never took her eyes off of mine. "There's something else. I talked to my husband. He knows that I am pregnant. Now, he's willing to give me a divorce." With the next words she searched my face. " The baby needs a father. If I marry again, I'll never get a divorce. It will be for the rest of my life."

She looked so beautiful, so filled with resolution that I wanted to reach out and take her in my arms. But I didn't. " I live in a small, one room place, with a mattress on the floor."

"I don't care where you live. Do you want me with you?"

"Yes." I answered and watched as tears started to form in her eyes. I moved closer to her, put my arms around her, and said, "I'm sorry; I was so stupid. The trouble is, I'm petrified. How the hell am I going to take care of a pregnant woman, when I can hardly take care of myself?"

"We'll do fine together. I'm going to have your baby."

* * * *

When the run of the play was over, I couldn't get work except at a gas station, then later at the L.A. Airport as an early morning ticket taker for one of the parking lots. But I got fired from that job, because I heard the cries of a stray cat that I found perched on the axle of a car. It was a kitten covered with grease. I took him into my small, heated ticket shack and fed him some milk. When the early morning traffic got busy, I lost track of the cat. When I found him, at the end of my shift, he had crawled in the back of a closed cupboard that held the different colored tickets for each day of the week. He was asleep on top of them and there was grease everywhere. When I showed what had happened to my boss, I was let go then and there. So here I was on my way home, with a grubby cat in the seat next to me, with no job, and an eight-month pregnant woman waiting to see me. I didn't know what I was going to tell her. We lived in Manhattan Beach now, in a little house where you could look through the boards called a floor and see the sand that the house was perched on. I decided to take the long way home. I went down El Segundo Boulevard toward the beach. When I passed the Standard Oil Refinery, there was a sign on a little building facing the street. It said, "Help Wanted." It was only eight o'clock in the morning, but it looked like the building was open. I left the cat and entered the building. There was one man behind a long counter.

"Hi." I said, "I noticed your sign."

"Have you got a college degree?" the man asked, peering intently at me. It looked as though the man expected lies.

"Yes, I do. San Jose State." I didn't plan on telling him my major. The man reached under the counter and brought out an employment form. " Fill this out and bring it back when you can."

"Could I fill it out now and leave it with you?"

"Sure, if you have time."

"What job is open?" I asked brightly.

"The Accounting Department is looking for a clerical."

Oh, great, I thought; something I know absolutely nothing about. "Oh, that's fine. Got a pen?" The form was filled with really strange questions. Such as, "Of the calculators listed below to which are you familiar?" Some of the names I couldn't even pronounce; they were German or from some foreign country. I didn't even know what they did, but I marked them like I knew them all. And so, it went throughout the form. Whatever they wanted to hear, I would agree. I didn't know what else to do. Aileen was eight months pregnant, and we had enough money for a week or two. I finished the form, handed it to the man, who said that someone would contact me within a week. Great, I thought. A week!

When I walked into the house with the kitten, Aileen asked where it came from and why it was so greasy? It was a perfect opening for the whole story. I put it out there not knowing what to expect from her. When I finished, she looked at me and said, "I'm glad. I don't like being alone in this place at night." Then she slowly got up, took an old towel and the kitten into the bathroom. Fifteen or twenty minutes later she came out with a clean kitten. He had a white chest and feet. The tip of his tail was white too. Everything else was black. "Let's call him 'Tuxy', Aileen said with a smile. Here we were having a baby in a month, and she was naming the cat that got me fired.

About eight-thirty the next morning I got a call from the Accounting Department at Standard Oil. The woman on the phone asked me if I could possibly be there by ten A.M.? I immediately agreed. As I hung up I thought, now I know that they are really in a hurry to get someone who knows what they're doing. I doubted if they wanted a desperate liar in their company. It didn't matter; I still had to try.

I got to the lobby of the main building a few minutes early, but the woman at the desk said to go down the hallway to the right and then into the second door. She said I would be speaking to Mr. Van Hom. I expected to walk into a singular office, but it was a large room with about fifteen or twenty men in white shirts and ties seated at separate desks. At the far side of the large room was a glass-enclosed area. The man sitting at the desk was hanging up the phone as he waved at me. I walked through all the men and up to his door

"Mr. Van Hom?"

"Yeah, that's me. Shut the door and have a seat." There were two wooden chairs. I sat in the first one. The man had a thin, angular face with a couple of liver spots on one side. He looked tired. He was looking down at my application. I waited.

"What was your major at San Jose?" He went right to the heart of it.

"Dramatic literature," I answered, waiting for the axe to fall.

"You're an actor, huh? Do you know Robert Redford?"

I almost laughed out loud I was so surprised at his question. "No, he's out of my league."

"Well, his dad is my boss." I didn't know how to continue the conversation in the direction it was going. I decided not to waste the man's time.

"Mister Van Hom, yesterday I was working at the L.A. Airport as a ticket taker, and I got fired. I've got a woman at home who is eight months pregnant, and on the way home to tell her the news, I saw your employment sign." Van Hom just kept looking at me. " I don't know how to work any of the machines out there in the office, and I've never had anything to do with accounting. I just needed a job, so I put down what I thought you wanted to see."

Van Hom continued to stare at me for another few moments, and then yelled, "Billy!" Startled, I looked behind me. One of the men got up from his desk and opened the door to Van Hom's office.

"Yes, Sir?"

"This is Robert. Teach him how to work the machines, and how to print numbers correctly." He grinned. "Actors have to eat too."

I almost went into tears, as I got up to follow Billy. "Thanks, Mister Van Hom; you're a life saver."

He smiled and said, "No, I'm not the life saver." I wondered what he meant and waited for more. None came. I followed Billy. The next few weeks I felt as though I was back in school. Even though it was a struggle I began to learn how accountants do what they do. I never fell in love with the job, but I was grateful and worked as diligently as I could.

On July 24th Aileen gave birth to a baby girl. We decided

upon the name Cara, which means, "loved one" in Gallic.

I worked for Standard Oil for five years. An incident happened in 1963 that I haven't forgotten. Mr. Van Hom had given me a new job that I'd been at for about five weeks. It carried me out into the refinery. Everyday I'd put on a hard-hat, grab the clipboard with the schematics on it, and go out the back door of the office building. My job was to mark down the ID numbers of each piece of equipment within each plant of the huge refinery. The company was in the process of putting all the equipment on a huge, newly purchased computer: every pump, every motor, storage tank, compressor and other things that I didn't even know the names of. It was my job to mark the identification numbers on the schematics that had been made up for each of the sections of the refinery. I couldn't miss one object within these separate areas. This one morning with my hard-hat on and clipboard in hand, I began to push open the back door of the building, when I was seized with a fear like I had never felt before. My hand started shaking, and my eyes seemed to lose their focus. I knew that I wasn't supposed to go out that door. I didn't know what to make of it, but I knew I couldn't go against it. I went back into the office and into Mr. Van Hom's office. As usual he was doing some paperwork. He looked up.

"I'm sorry Mister Van Hom but I can't go out into the

yard today."

"Why not?"

I told him what had happened at the door. Van Hom paused for a moment, then said, "Then you don't go. Find something to do at your desk." I thanked him and did as I was told. An hour or so later there was an explosion that was loud enough to be heard in the office. I looked up at Van Hom's office and saw that he was looking at me. Then the boss picked up his phone. I never took my eyes off of him as he had a short conversation with someone. He hung up the phone, got out of his chair and came over to my desk. "An explosion took place where you were supposed to be today. A valve had been shut that was supposed to be open." He paused. "Nobody was hurt." He looked a long moment at me, then turned and went back to his office. I sat there in a stupor, wondering how such a thing could happen to me.

CHAPTER SIX

A Strange Occurrence

In the early part of 1964, Art, my step-grandfather had a heart attack. I was with him when he had it. We were looking at car parts, and he thought that he was having bad gas pains. But he found out what he had, and during that year his heart became weaker and weaker. The large, gentle man became bed-ridden.

In November, Aileen, Cara, who was now three, and I went to Bellflower to visit with Art and Mother Jerry. Aunt Violet, who was now divorced again, had moved from New Jersey and was living in Long Beach. When I came into the house, I was carrying Cara, and I saw that Violet was there visiting too. The two of them were seated in the living room.

"How's Art?" I asked. While I was asking this question, I remembered a few years before, when I was in college, Mother Jerry confided with me that Art didn't know how to read, and would I teach him. He always wanted to learn, but he never talked about it. He was too embarrassed. I told Mother Jerry I didn't have the time. I had thought about Art since his heart attack, and what I hadn't done for the man.

"He's probably sleeping." Mother Jerry answered. Aileen stayed in the living room with the two of them, so with Cara on my arm, I said, "I think we'll go and say hello, if he's awake." I walked down the hallway, knocked gently on the door, then opened it. As it opened, a moment passed, then I felt something shockingly cold go through my body. I peered at Art in his bed and knew he was dead. I slightly tightened my grip on Cara, as if to protect her, then turned and walked back into the living room.

"Mother Jerry, Art's dead," I said quietly, not wanting to frighten Cara.

" What! He...he can't be!" Mother Jerry said as she passed us. Violet followed, screaming as she went. Aileen had stood but was now still, looking at me.

"I'm going to take her outside," I said.

Aileen nodded, and then I opened the front door. I could

hear screaming now. I shut the door, walked down the porch stairs, and then down the street. I walked, holding Cara, until the ambulance came and took the body away.

(Years later, when Cara was married and had three children, she said that she had seen two grandpas at that time in the bedroom, one in bed and the other walking toward them. She too remembered the coldness passing through her.)

* * *

CHAPTER SEVEN

Life was Good

After the birth of Cara, my wife had decided that she didn't like the way the hospital provided assistance for the birth, feeling that they were more interested in their protocol and their own priorities than the birthing mother. She read "Child Birth Without Fear" and decided she would have her second one at home. Through a friend she found a doctor who would deliver at our home. On July 23rd of '67, Doctor Eddinghausen was there, and as the child was coming out of the birth canal, the doctor said quietly that the umbilical cord was wrapped around the baby's neck three times. Her pretty little face was a deep blue as she came out, so the doctor clamped and cut the umbilical cord, releasing her to be fully birthed. She wasn't breathing. But the doctor was very calm as he firmly hit her backside until she gasped and began crying. Right away, the doctor handed the baby to Aileen. I was so exhausted watching this whole ordeal that I felt as though I had had the baby.

Cara, who was to be six years old the next day on the 24th, had gone around the neighborhood and gathered all her friends. They were waiting in the living room. When everything was cleaned and put in order, I went out and told all the kids that they could come in and see the new baby girl. None of the kids had seen a person so new. They were quiet and in awe as they first looked at the baby, and then smiled at Aileen. I knew that it was a new experience for all of them and me. Cara spoke up and said her new sister was to be called "Meghan."

(An interesting side issue for the day was that Cara and I had tickets for the Circus that same day for her birthday. After Meghan's birth, Aileen said for the two of us to go ahead and enjoy ourselves. When we got back to the house that evening, Aileen was up and had made dinner for us, with the help of her mother.)

In 1969, a friend of mine and a good director in Hollywood called and asked if I would like to go to Yugoslavia to be in one of his movies. Needless to say, I accepted. After three weeks there, I came home, and our third child was conceived. On July 9th we had a boy. We named him Shannon. He was a big guy, 23 inches long and eleven pounds. He was born at home too, with his Grandma present.

In the seventies, I left Standard Oil and became a salesman for Harper and Row Publishers. My territory was Southern California, New Mexico and El Paso, Texas. I wasn't much for traveling, so my job didn't last that long, even though they were a good company to work for. Next, I went to work in Los Angeles for a department store chain as their book buyer. I was getting heavy around the waist, so instead of taking the elevator, I'd walked the stairs. After a couple of weeks, I was running up to the fourth floor where my office was. It wasn't enough to help the waistline, so I started jogging down at The Strand, (a wide cement walkway that ran along the beaches of Manhattan and Hermosa). I'd run in the evenings when it wasn't so crowded. It took me a few months, but I got up to about five miles and did my best to get down there four or five times a week.

A couple of other job changes took place that led to Aileen and I having our own business. We had a shop in Redondo Beach, just a few miles from our home in Manhattan Beach. We were picture framers and sold wholesale to a large chain of stores throughout the United States.

Life was good. I thought things were the way they ought to be. Our children were all in school, and we gave them as much freedom as we could, which was supposedly the "hip

Summerhill" way in the 70's.

We also smoked grass, my wife and I, and grew a little of it too. There were times when I was hard on my children, too hard when they didn't do what they were supposed to do. I remember back in 1969, I quit smoking after twenty-five years. When I would come home, my two girls were so frightened at the way I acted that they would go hide in the closet when they heard my car coming into the garage. Giving up on this habit brought out my anger, enough so that it even surprised me. That wasn't the only time I was hard on my children, only that I remember it well.

My anger ran further than just my children. I had a business partner in part of my work with our framing company. He had a product that he made. My wife designed the framing for it, and then our company did the framing and shipping to our clients. In 1978, he told us that he was no longer going to work with us. No explanation, it was just over. We probably saw a quarter of a million dollars gone. Since our contract, if you want to call it that, was just verbal with a handshake, I could do nothing about it. I could only simmer.

CHAPTER EIGHT

In the Blink of An Eye – Life Changed

On October 18th, 1978 I left my office a little early and was on my way home to change and go down to the Strand for my run. When I pulled up in front of the house, Shannon, my eight-year-old son, was sitting on the doorstep.

"Hi, son. What's up?" He looked a little solemn.

"Nothin."

"I'm going for my run. I'll be home in plenty of time to get you to the baseball sign ups."

"O.K." He just sat there.

I went into the house. Cara, my eldest child was sitting on the sofa reading. "What's wrong with Shannon?" I asked.

"Nothing. Is he still out on the front porch?"

I went in to the bedroom and changed into my jogging shorts, a loose tee shirt and my running shoes. When I came outside my son was still sitting there. It was unlike him. "Are you sure you're all right?"

"Sure. I'm fine."

I got into the van, started it up. Shannon was still looking at me. I waved, and he waved back.

Sometimes, when I got to the beach, it was difficult to find a parking space. But not this time, right on First Street, facing away from the ocean was the last parking space. I pulled the van in and got out. I didn't have any pockets in my running shorts, but I had purchased a little Velcro pocket that fit neatly on my tennis shoe. I put the car key in it, and walked to the wall that separated the Strand from the beach. I put one leg on the wall and slowly bent, stretching the muscles of the other leg, then the other. As I stretched I decided which way I was going to run. The day before I had run north to the Manhattan Beach Pier, then south, past the van and down to the Hermosa Pier, then back to the van. This time I would do just the opposite. I started with an easy jog, warming up, usually for the first mile or so. Then I would lengthen my stride and pick up the pace for the next four miles.

Since it was October and late in the afternoon, the Strand wasn't crowded, and the weather was good, there was a light breeze and it was maybe in the high sixties. At the slow pace, I reached the Hermosa Pier. As I turned, I decided to pick up the tempo until I reached the Manhattan Pier, about 2 miles.

[The next portion of the story, even though I'm writing it, is being told mostly by my wife, and also by a few people I did not know before or couldn't remember.]

I was just about to pass a man who was seated on the wall that separated the sand from The Strand. He saw me come out of my run, stiffen until I was straight, my mouth wide open, my eyes opened wider, and I fell forward, my face hitting the cement. He later told my wife that he didn't even come over to the body because he knew I was dead. He ran into his skate-rental shop and called the Paramedics. (He also later told her that he wondered why he was still sitting there on the wall because all the skates were returned already. He could have gone home whenever he wanted.) After his call, when he came out of the shop, there was a small crowd gathered around my body.

At the same time the man was phoning, there was another man running behind me, and saw me fall. He rolled me over and was going to give me mouth-to-mouth resuscitation, but he could see that my front upper teeth where gone and were probably lodged in my throat. He began pushing in on my chest, giving me CPR. He looked up at the group around him.

"Has anybody called the paramedics?"

The small crowd looked at one another, but no one knew what to say.

It happened that two paramedics were playing tennis just a few blocks from The Strand. They arrived at the Strand in a few minutes. Paul Zavala, in his late twenties, was the first over my body. He carried the case with the electric paddles. When he bent over me, the man who had been giving me CPR got to his feet and began running down The Strand. He knew I was dead and that I probably didn't stand a chance. He felt he hadn't done a thing to help.

Paul decided to rip my tee shirt and put the paddles to my chest, but then saw that my upper teeth had ripped out of my gums and were down my throat.

"Bring the suction machine!" He yelled at his partner.

With it, he reached into my throat and brought out the broken teeth. Then he ripped away my tee shirt, put the paddles on my chest and pulled the trigger. My body jumped, then I started breathing again. The other paramedic (I never knew his name) rolled the gurney up, and he and Paul started to lift me on to it. When they touched me, I began screaming and became violent, lashing out at them. Fortunately, by this time, two lifeguards had come from the station on the Pier. They helped and got me onto the gurney, strapped me down and slid me into the paramedic van.

Once inside, I died again. Paul quickly put the paddles across my chest and fired them again, but this time they didn't work. He tried again. Nothing!

"He's gone again, and the paddles won't work!" he shouted to his partner who was now driving. "I have to go through the artery!" (A plastic tube would pierce the throat into the main artery running into the heart. Once in, then epinephrine would be shot directly into the heart chamber.)

"You have to call the hospital and get permission for that!" his partner answered.

Paul knew this and called the doctor on duty. The doctor said, "No," wait until he gets here, and he'd take care of it. Paul knew it would be too late. He had never done the procedure before, only seen it on the screen in a drawn diagram. The danger was if done incorrectly, the patient could bleed to death internally.

He picked up the plastic tubing, with its end sharpened like a razor. As he did, he told my wife later, that it felt as though someone was guiding his hand. The plastic tube cut the throat at just the right angle, and it entered the artery. Paul guided it into the heart. Once in, he pressed the syringe at the end of the tube and watched as the liquid traveled into the throat. Moments later, my heart started, and I gasped for breath. They were just entering the driveway of the hospital.

CHAPTER NINE

Where's Dad?

My son had been sitting on the steps to the front door, waiting for me. He got up and went to his mother, who had come home from the shop. "Dad's real late," he said to her. (I should have been home a half-hour to forty-five minutes earlier.) He stood still before Aileen, with a worried look on his face.

"Maybe we should go and look for him," she said.

Shannon agreed, and they both went to the garage then drove down to the beach. She knew where I usually parked the van, and there it was. She parked near to it, then she and Shannon stood on the Strand wondering which way I had gone. Aileen decided to go toward the Manhattan Pier. As they walked, Aileen asked people if they had seen a tall, gray-hair man jogging. First, they walked, toward the Manhattan Beach Pier, then turned and walked past the cars toward the Hermosa

Pier. She kept asking everyone she saw on The Strand, but with no success. Just before she got back to her car, she stopped.

"We need a phone." She turned and looked at the corner house. There were lights on. She went to the door. She knocked first, waited a few moments, then saw the doorbell and pressed it.

"There's someone in there. I can see them moving around." Shannon said, as he looked through the front window. "And the lights are going on and off."

A few more moments passed, and a man answered the door. Aileen started to speak, but the man gestured with his hand, and said, "I'm sorry; I'm deaf. You'll have to come in, so I can see your face." Both she and Shannon entered the man's living room. The man watched intently as Aileen slowly spoke.

"We've been searching for my husband, but can't find him. May I use your phone?" As she spoke she gestured by lifting her hand to her ear.

"Yes, of course." He motioned toward the phone. Aileen went to it and dialed the operator. "Yes, operator, this is an emergency. Could you connect me with the Manhattan Beach Police Department?" A slight pause, then, "Thank you." Aileen waited until an officer came on the phone. "Officer, I'm down on The Strand looking for my husband. Has there been any reports of any kind?" The officer told her that he heard over the intercom that a man "went down" near the Hermosa Pier and that they took him to the South Bay Hospital. Aileen tried to keep her countenance as calm as possible, because she could see Shannon staring up at her. " Would you have the phone number?" she asked. There was a pencil and a piece of paper on the small table near the phone. She wrote the number down. "Thank you, officer." She hung up and dialed.

"Hello, I'm calling about a man the police department said went down on The Strand. Is that right?"

"Yes, a little less than an hour ago," the nurse answered.

"Is he 6 feet four with gray hair?"

"Yes, he is." A pause followed.

"Could I ask you, what kind of a car does he drive?"

"A Ford van."

"Then this might be him. A Ford key was the only thing

found, and it was attached to his running shoe."

"Did you notice if he had scars on his stomach? They're from operations he had when he was little."

A pause followed, and then the nurse said, " Yes, he does." Then a longer pause. "The doctor suggests that you don't drive to the hospital; either go with a friend or take a taxi." Aileen said thanks as she hung up. She nodded, thanking the deaf man for the use of his phone, then took Shannon's hand and went quickly to the car. She drove him home. Once she was inside, she told Cara that I was in the hospital.

"What happened?" Cara asked.

"The only thing I know, is that he 'went down' by the Hermosa Pier." Neither of them knew what to say. "Watch after the kids. I don't know what time I'll be home."

Aileen sat in the car for a moment, though she knew where the hospital was. In a way, she was afraid to go. She had noticed how Shannon hadn't said a word on the way home, and neither had she. She turned the key on and moved toward Prospect Avenue.

When Aileen asked for the ICU and said who she was, the nurse at the desk sent her up to the third floor. When the elevator door opened, the doctor was there, waiting for her. He wanted to talk to her before she went in to see him.

"Your husband collapsed with a heart attack down on The Strand. As far as we can tell, he was dead for about four to four and a half minutes before the paramedics got to him. They revived him, but when they put him into the van, he died again. The paramedic thought maybe four minutes again, Mrs.?"

"McNamara," Aileen responded.

"I should caution you about your husband's fall. His face landed on the cement. His front teeth were ripped out, and his chin area is highly lacerated."

"May I go see him now?" Aileen asked quietly.

"Yes, of course. A nurse will take you to his room."

"Thank you."

The doctor motioned to the nurse behind the counter who went toward the room with Aileen following.

The room was small with a single bed, all types of machines and two chairs. A male nurse was seated near the head of bed. He smiled, stood up, and gave her the chair. The other chair was at the end of the bed. He sat there. Aileen noticed immediately that I was in restraints, leather bands around my wrists and ankles attached to the sides of the bed. She looked at the nurse.

"When we took him out of the paramedic van and tried to transfer him from their gurney to ours . . . I had his right arm. As I started to lift him, he grabbed me and threw me over the gurney and against the wall. He was screaming the whole time. We finally restrained him and took him up here. We had the same problem getting him from our gurney into the bed."

Aileen didn't know what to say. She looked at all the attachments to my body, plastic drips, lines to different machines, and a breathing mask over my nose and mouth. She started to take my hand, but thought better of it.

The male nurse came and went, depending on what he had to do. Aileen was alone with me and had been in the room for maybe two hours, when suddenly my eyes opened as I sat upright (as far as I could move), the mask pulling away from my face, and I screamed, "Help me, God, help me!!!! Help me! Oh,

God, help me!!" Over and over again I screamed it, until the night nurse came in and intravenously gave me a shot of Valium.

"That should calm him." He went back to the desk.

It did, but only for about twenty or thirty minutes. Over and over again for the next ten hours, I screamed out for God to help me. Aileen told me later that she had never heard anyone scream with such terror and complete abandonment. Once in a while, she said, I would say in a childlike voice, "Daaaaddy...Daaaaddy, help me, Daddy."

In the morning, when I was awake, I kept asking my wife "Who took my teeth? What did I do wrong?" She would try to soothe me by telling me that I had an accident down on The Strand. But then I would forget what she said, and asked the same questions over and over again.

The morning nurse came in while I was asking my wife. She looked directly at me and said, "You had a heart attack, and you were dead for a few minutes." When she said it, I went into such a panic that I could hardly breathe, and I screamed again and again, "What!? Whaaaat!?" Over and over again, with complete abandonment and terror, and then I started crying. My wife told me she did her best to soothe me, but it didn't take long before I forgot what the nurse had told me and I started asking the same old questions again. My wife also told me that I kept thanking the nurses and the doctor over and over again.

The next day when my wife went home to make sure the children were alright, she wondered if she was going to have to live with this man as he was now. How would she do it? That day she brought our oldest daughter, Cara, to see me. I didn't know who she was.

A couple of days later they moved me from ICU into a regular room in the Cardiac Unit. I had a roommate, but there was a drawn curtain between us most of the time.

From time to time, Paul Zavala, the paramedic, would come into my room to say hello. I later found out that he came in " to check me out". He couldn't believe that I wasn't a "squash head". (Normally when you've been dead as long as I had, your brain, because of the lack of oxygen, doesn't come back to normal, and you become what most call a vegetable.)

On the fourth morning (I think that was the day) I was awakened by a very strong tingling sensation in my toes. It started going into my feet and then my legs. I panicked, looking at the oscilloscope, even though I didn't understand any of the apparatus connected to me. I thought I was having another heart attack. The sensation continued through my stomach, my chest cavity, my neck and my head. When it got to my head, I knew that I was all right! I don't know how I knew it, but I was sure of it. When the doctor showed up in the afternoon, I excitedly told him about it. He looked at me for a moment, then said, "That's fine, but later we'll still give you a stress test, just in case." Later, I told my wife the same story, and she looked at me the way the doctor had.

CHAPTER TEN

Changes in Me

My wife told me that one of the strangest things I did while in the hospital was to ask her to bring me a Bible. She couldn't believe it, but after I asked her four or five times, she said she would. When she brought the Bible, I found that I couldn't read it, because the death experience had affected my eyes, made everything close to me look blurry. I would have to wait until I got home, saw an optometrist, then I could read it. As the Book stayed near my bed, I would glance at it, wondering why I had asked my wife for it. Sometimes I wondered who it belonged to.

I hadn't been awake for very long one morning, when a woman in a beautiful bathrobe was standing alongside my bed. She smiled at me, and I smiled back.

She said hello and then said, "I heard that you were dead for a while?"

"Yes, that's what they tell me."

"I think I'm supposed to tell you a story. Would you mind?" she said softly.

"No," I answered. She sat in the chair next to the bed.

"I was giving birth to my third child, when I died. I left my body and was up in the corner of the room watching the doctor and nurses working frantically over me. Suddenly, I left the room and was in a bright tunnel going upwards. And then I was in a beautiful meadow with the greenest grass, and the most beautiful flowers I'd ever seen. In the middle of the meadow was a stone wall, and in the wall, was a wooden gate. Standing on the other side of the gate was my grandmother. She's the one who brought me to the Lord. I walked through the grass, and we were hugging each other over the wooden gate. I could understand her thoughts as we hugged. I started to open up the gate, and she said to me, "No, child, you have to go back and raise your three children." And suddenly, I was back in my body and felt a slight pain as the doctor administered a drug in my arm."

She was smiling at me, and yet for some reason I cried through the entire story. I don't remember when she left, but I couldn't stop crying.

Later, when the doctor came, I told him the story. He looked at me for a moment after I had finished, then said, "This hospital hasn't had birthing services for over two years." He smiled, and I didn't know what to say. Though I don't remember very much of what happened in the hospital, I've never forgotten the story, but I can't remember the face of the woman.

Some days later, a Catholic priest came through the door, paused and smiled at me. Because of my time at a Catholic military school, I could not abide either priests or nuns. And yet, I found myself smiling at him as he asked me if this was the correct room for whatever my roommate's name was. Why did I smile at the man with the white collar? I nodded to the priest to go on the other side of the curtain, that's where the Catholic was. I examined inside myself and found that I really did mean the smile when I gave it. I questioned my sanity as I thought about it.

There was another strange phenomenon that took place in me. Usually, I would think, when you have a heart attack, die, fall flat on your face, and end up in a hospital, you would feel pretty lousy about the whole thing. But I didn't. I felt something new within me and each night when I went to sleep, I would hope that this new "feeling" would still be there. This feeling was something like a calmness or a peacefulness that I had never felt before. I thought maybe it was the drugs I was being given.

I really didn't know what it was, but I didn't want it to go away. Each morning when I woke, the first thing I did was to check this new feeling out, to make sure it was still there. It didn't take much, just lie there and feel what was going on inside. I was always fearful about losing it, but every morning it was there. I never talked to anybody about this, because I didn't know how to explain it. I didn't want people looking at me like I might be crazy. If this was crazy, then I wanted to keep it forever.

For the last few days in the hospital, two nurses had been helping me walk up and down the hallway. They were little ladies. I felt sorry for them, because I had to lean so much of my weight on them. Then after fifteen days the doctor said it was time to go home. He told me to begin walking on my own, not too much at first, but it was necessary to build up my strength. Aileen got me home, and I got out of the car and made my way into the house, I was exhausted. Aileen told me, I went right to bed.

CHAPTER ELEVEN

Home Again

Two or three days later, she took me to the optometrist and then in a couple of days I would have my glasses. Then I took my first walk. I don't think I'll ever forget it. Our house was in the middle of the block, which had a slope to it, and as I stood on our front porch, I decided to take the sidewalk down the hill. I got three houses away and had to stop. I looked back at our house and knew that I was going to have to rest before I could make it up the hill.

I sat down on the lawn, then I decided to lie down. An hour or two later, the lady of the house woke me up. Even with sleep, I felt so weak, that a portion of my walk turned into a crawl. I'd always taken my strength for granted. But now, going from jogging five miles a day to crawling into my house, changed my mind as to who I was. I had the strength of a sick little baby. It seemed to me that everything in my life had changed.

Some days later, I went and tried on my glasses. I read the plastic covered page they put in front of me. I had no trouble reading the smallest print at the very bottom.

The next morning, after my children went to school and my wife went to our business, I sat at our kitchen table with a Bible in front of me. As I looked down at it, I remembered when I was the book buyer for the department store chain in Los Angeles. Every year I would travel to Washington D.C. for the American Booksellers Association. All the publishers had booths, and buyers from all over the world would come and browse the coming publications. Nighttime's were boring. I wasn't a drinker and didn't like to travel in a city I didn't know, so would stay in my hotel room. Most of the times, I had a book or two from the publishers that knew me and would read at night. But once in a while, I'd be stuck in the room with a T.V. and find most of the programs repetitious and filled with boredom. Then I'd open up the drawer to the little nightstand next to the bed and see the Gideon Bible. I'd take out the red, hardcover book and arbitrarily open it. Whatever page I would be on, I'd read it. Each time I read it I'd have the same reaction of shaking my head in disbelief. I would toss the Book back in the drawer wondering why anyone felt this tangled mass of words important.

Now I sat looking down at it. It was an expensive Bible that I had received from the Oxford University Press. I didn't have to pay for it, nor did I have to pay for the few thousand books I had scattered throughout shelves built in our house. This was a thick one, a study Bible, so I attempted to read it. It had been in my top bookshelf for some years, because I never attempted to even look at it. Suddenly, it occurred to me that I should look up and see what the Book had to say about hell.

Such a thought surprised me, because I didn't know what else to look up. So, I did it. In the back of the Book they had an area called "Concise Concordance". I found the word "hell" in it, but also other words that meant the same: Sheol, Hades, the Pit and Torment. I think I decided to look in Matthew first, because it used the word "hell". So, I wrote down all the numbers from that Concordance. It took me a while, but I finally found Matthew, the first book in the New Testament. For some reason the lettering I was reading was in red. As I read the words, I was startled, because I knew exactly what they meant! There weren't any of my old thoughts that entered my head. I knew what they meant, and I knew they were true!

I started crying. I couldn't help it. Then when I tried to

think about what I had just read, I couldn't remember what I had just read. And during the next few hours that I read from the Bible, I found that nothing changed. I cried but couldn't remember. I think I fell asleep at the table, but I'm not sure of that. In those days, and weeks, I wasn't sure about anything.

In time, my walking got longer, a few blocks and then a half-mile. Sometimes I'd have to sit down before starting home, but as far as I can remember I didn't fall asleep in somebody's yard again.

Sometimes, I would write things down from the Bible, things that really excited me, and then I would read them to my family at dinnertime. After reading it, I would look at them and know that I had made a mistake. They didn't understand or care about what I was reading. Cara, who was now seventeen, thought I was crazy. I could tell by the look on her face. Without a word, she would get up from the table and go to her room.

As I continued to read during the days, I began to understand why I read what I did. Though I didn't remember, I knew that I had been in hell. Some thoughts kept coming to me over and over again. One, I had lost my free will when I died. I had no choice. Second, I knew, without any doubts, that there was an afterlife. Thirdly, and the most frightening to me, I now know there is a God, and that down there I would forever be without Him.

I questioned how these thoughts came to me, but I knew without hesitation that they were true. Though I didn't understand my tears when I read what I did, I never tried to stop them. I also "felt" that I had been in a terrible darkness, and that the darkness became increasingly frightening as I stayed in it.

(When the movie "Ghost" came out in 1990, my wife and I went to see it. When the demons came out of the underworld and took hold of Tony Goldwyn's and his Mexican accomplice's souls and drug them down into the depths of the Earth, I involuntarily shuddered. Once again, I knew something without hesitation; this was true. It's what happened to me and that's why I fought the paramedics and the male nurse when they touched my arms. I thought I was still being dragged down, still being held by demons. During the movie, my wife took my hand and moved as close as she could to me. Now, she knew what had happened too.)

But back to 1979. By March I was walking a few miles every other day. Sometimes I would go to our place of business and say hello to everyone. When I did, I would walk through the parking lot of a church, which was about half way between our house and business. Sometimes, when I crossed through it in the mornings, I would see this short, white-haired man climbing the stairs to the back entrance to the church. If he saw me, he would acknowledge me with a smile and walk on. I guessed he must have been the priest or pastor, whatever he was called, because he was always dressed nicely.

One morning when I got to our business, I was a little more tired than usual. I went into the building, sat in the chair by the phone and promptly fell asleep. When I woke up, my face was turned toward the side wall of the room. There usually were a couple of pictures hanging on the wall, ones that my wife liked. But now, as I looked, on the floor, leaning against the wall were a group of framed pictures, all the same size, stacked one against the other. I could only see the first one, but I stared at it. I couldn't make it out except that it was in black and white and the group of people seemed to be dressed in old-fashioned clothes.

I went over and picked one up. It was my mother's family. I took it to my desk, sat down, and stared at it. My mother and Violet were in the front row. My mother had on a white dress and was about two years old. Both the girls had white ribbons in their hair, and Violet had this very large doll with a hat on that was bigger than the girls' bows. Mother Jerry and her husband, Shady, were standing behind them. Shady had a bowler hat tipped precariously to one side – very dapper. Mother Jerry had a long dark gown on that ran all the way up to her shoulders, then around her neck with black lace. She had a white handkerchief in her left hand. I would say that she was in her mid-twenties and was beautiful. To her left were her two brothers, my great uncles. To Shady's right was Mother Jerry's father. The picture was taken in front of a mass of tall bramble bushes with leaves strewn on the ground. It must have been fall in Texas.

Now for the reason I bring up this small incident. As I looked at my grandmother, it flashed on me, enough to startle me, the words she had spoken to me at the kitchen table, when I stayed in the little trailer, "Bobby, you're going to be surprised at what is going to happen to you. I pray for you every day of your life." I started crying, as I did when reading the Word. I didn't try to stop. I think I fell back to sleep.

*Editor's Note: (No doubt this grandmother's prayers changed things for Robert and continued to save him throughout his life and the heart attack. Prayer changes things!)

CHAPTER TWELVE

What Do I Have to Do?

Because of the loss of my short term memory, one thought seemed to occur to me over and over again. Since I went to hell, and now I'm back, before I die again, what do I have to do so I won't go back again? I did read a section from the book of Joel, *"And it shall come to pass that whosoever shall call on the name of the LORD shall be delivered."* From what my wife told me, I certainly called on His name over and over again. Was that enough? The feeling I had within me since I was in the hospital was that I wouldn't go back down there, but I didn't know whether to trust my feelings or not. I needed more information. I decided to go to church.

I told my wife and children about my decision. My wife looked at me for a moment, then said, "Good. Why not?" The children seemed to agree with her, but I could tell that none of them were thinking about going with me. So, the next Sunday I got ready. I decided to go to the church with the parking lot that I knew. I stopped short. As many times as, I walked by the church and looked at their glass-covered bulletin board, I couldn't remember when the service started. When I got there, I saw that I was forty-five minutes early. When the people started coming, they all brought their Bibles. I didn't even think to bring mine.

I went through the main door, standing next to it, was a smiling man who stuck out his hand to me. "Hi, I'm Harvey. Have you been here before?"

"No," I answered, not mentioning the knowledge I had of the church's parking lot.

"Well, let me show you to a seat." He led me into the main room. It was large and about half full. "Would you like to sit in the front?"

"No," I answered. "The back will be fine." He led me to the second to the last row of wooden pews, and I sat right next to the aisle. As I waited, more people came in. The church probably held five to six hundred people. Over my head, approximately a quarter of the way toward the stage area was a balcony.

A lady came out on stage, then down some stairs to a

piano. Then the little white-haired man I had seen climbing the stairs came on the stage and stood behind the pulpit. He was the pastor alright. Then a dozen or so men and women came from both sides of the stage and stood on two wooden platforms near the back of the stage. The pastor told us what page to turn to in the hymnal. I looked at the back of the pew in front of me and saw two of them in a wooden holder. I passed. The pianist started, the choir sang and so did the people in the audience. The songs were nice, about praising God and other good things I don't remember. The pastor sang with a lot of gusto, and he had a pretty good voice. After the songs, the choir came down the stairs and sat in the two front rows. Then some men came forward and passed some baskets through the rows collecting money for the church. I passed again. Then the pastor opened his Bible and everyone around me did the same thing. After he had opened it, he looked up, smiling slightly, and searched the audience. His gaze fell on me and stayed there for a moment as he began his sermon. He apologized to the audience as to what he was going to talk about, but he said it had been a long, long time since he had talked on hell and the ramifications of sin.

During the sermon, he must have looked directly at me four or five times. I wondered how he knew so much about hell when he hadn't been there. But as he talked my memory could not contain all that he was saying. After he had finished, the people began singing another song. I left during the song. Even though I knew it wasn't possible, I felt as though that pastor knew exactly where I'd been.

When I got home, I didn't talk about church, and they didn't ask any questions. I didn't go back to church for three weeks, and then Easter came. The day before Aileen said that she and the two younger children wanted to go to church with me. That night she got stoned and watched "Jesus Christ Super Star". I don't remember if I watched it with her or not.

A character-trait of my wife should be mentioned. In our business or any other relationships with other people, "integrity" was the utmost importance to her. If a person that we dealt with in business did not have integrity, she would no longer deal with them, even if in the long run it would cost us money. If a man did not give attention to his wife, but instead gave too much attention to her, then she would have nothing to do with him. She had been that way since I met her.

Easter morning, we got there a little early, and it was fortunate that we did. The place filled up and even the balcony was full. My family and I, without our eldest daughter, Cara, sat near the back, but a few pews closer than before. The choir seemed a little bit larger, and I wondered if it was because it was

Easter. After we sang, and the pastor said a prayer over us, he began his sermon. He spoke about the integrity of Christ and how He would have never gone through what He did unless He had a completeness in who He was and what His purpose was. When he finished, there was a moment of silence as he looked around the entire room and the balcony. Then he asked everyone to stand.

"If there are any of you here who have not received Christ as your Lord and Savior and would like to, please come forward," the pastor asked.

As I was looking around the room, I felt movement behind me. I looked to my right, where my wife was supposed to be, but she wasn't there. I looked to my left, and she was standing in the aisle, with tears streaming down her cheeks. She had her hand out toward me. She wanted me to go forward with her. I did. We held hands as we said, what I later found out, was the "Sinner's Prayer." I also found out later that we had responded to an "altar call". New Christians do this to show their commitment to Christ. I liked the idea. Even though I had never said it before, the Sinner's Prayer, didn't seem foreign to me. I already found out I was a sinner and had no trouble at all in knowing what a self-centered jerk I'd been for the past forty-eight years. When the pastor said that as sinners, my wife and I needed a Savior, and Jesus Christ was the man, I seemed to already know that. Him dying the way He did, and then being raised from the dead, I already believed that. Why wouldn't I? I already went to where non-believers go.

We started going to this church on Sunday mornings and evenings, Wednesday nights and any other time when something was going on. It was the first time my wife and I had so many friends.

A few weeks later, we got baptized. There was a baptismal behind curtains in the very back of the stage. I know that my wife and I said a few words before we were immersed, but I don't remember what was said. But then Meghan, my eleven-year-old daughter got immersed; I remember what she said.

"I got saved about a year and a half ago at a Vacation Bible Study at a friend's house. I never told my parents, because I knew how mad they would get."

The congregation laughed, and so did Aileen and I. My daughter was right. I would have been mad at her.

About a year went by when the pastor asked me if Aileen

and I would give our testimony. I thought maybe he would be traveling, but that night he was there, sitting in the front row. It took us about forty-five minutes to complete it. Afterward, when Aileen and I were coming off the stage area, a man sobbing with tears streaming from his eyes, went up to Aileen and said, "I was there! I was there!" She asked if he was the lifeguard that came from the Hermosa Pier.

"No, I was jogging behind him and saw him fall. The Lord told me the man was married and had children. I went up to him, rolled him over and tried to give him mouth-to-mouth resuscitation, but his teeth were down his throat. The only thing I could do was giving him CPR until the paramedics got there. As soon as they came, I left. I knew he was dead. I didn't think he had a chance."

"Do you go to our church?" Aileen asked.

"No. I've never been here before. My church is showing a movie I'd already seen. I'd heard that the pastor here was a good speaker, so I came to hear him." He didn't stop crying. "I thought I had failed to help."

God is unbelievable in the wondrous things He does. He cared about the way the man felt, and He wanted to straighten him out. Later, I called Paul Zavala, the paramedic and asked him when he got to me if I was on my stomach or my back?

"You were on your stom... No, wait a minute, you were on your back! I didn't have to roll you."

I told him what had happened at the church. Then he said, "Now I understand why you aren't a "squash-head." There are a few other points I'd like to cover.

About my father: Aileen and I have forgotten the year, but we went over to the Sunnyside Mausoleum and paid for my father's name being put on his crypt. A few months later we went back over and looked at it. The size was right, and it looked nice.

About my grandmother: Through the years, I've thought more about her, a great deal more. When I was six days old, she saved my life. When I was eight, she did it again. Then, when I was forty-eight, her years of consistency in prayer, I believe, saved my life and brought a waiting God into my life. I would never have thought that when I screamed out for God to help me, that my soul was what He cared about. When I went to hell, I thought all of me was down there. And that all of me was my body, because I didn't know or believe that human beings have souls. How little I knew. I also know now that it was God who put me on my Grandmother's heart. I believe she knew that and would never give up on something that God had given her. I'll say thank you to her over and over again when I see her, and give her a big hug, which I have never given her.

About our son Shannon: When he was ten years old he went to a children's group at our church called, "AWANA" (Approved workman are not ashamed). One evening at the AWANA gathering, one of the leaders led my son in the Sinner's Prayer.

About my daughter, Cara, the bright one. She left home after high school, and ended up living with a young man up in Stockton, California. They'd been together for a while, and he had a heavy history. He'd been in prison, and told Cara that he killed somebody. I'd told the church about this, and we'd been praying for her for about a year. Then at 2 A.M. in the morning, we were wakened with a phone call. Aileen answered the phone call. It was Cara. She was crying.

"Mom, John told me to come home, but I couldn't. I didn't have a ride, and we had to work late. John put my clothes in a duffle bag and put them in the middle of the living room. I took it and went to a friend's house."

"Does he know where you are?" Aileen asked

"No, he doesn't."

"If he found you and killed you, what would happen to your soul?"

"I'd go to hell, wouldn't I Mama?" Cara said through her tears. "Yes, you would. Do you think you ought to accept the Lord now?"

"Yes, Mama."

"Repeat after me."

"Jesus Christ is the Son of God, and He died for our sins. I accept Him as my Lord and Savior. Come into my heart right now, Lord Jesus. Amen."

Cara repeated the words she heard her mother say, "What are you going to do now?" Aileen asked.

"I want to get on a bus and come home."

"Call us before you leave and tell us when you'll get into Los Angeles. Daddy will pick you up."

She called and a friend from church and I met her down in Los Angeles. We drove home. It was good to have her there.

We'd been home about an hour when the phone rang. I answered it and a male voice asked if Cara was there. I said yes and handed the phone to our daughter.

Then he said to her. " What are you doing down there?!"

"I got your message when I saw my clothes packed in the front room." "Your clothes?! Did you look in the bag?"

"No."

"Well look!"

Cara got the bag and dumped it upside down. The bottom of the bag was filled with John's clothes. She picked up the phone.

"What is this?" she asked.

"It's the dirty clothes. I wanted you to do the laundry. That's all."

So, our daughter got saved because of a bag of dirty clothes God is wonderful and has a sense of humor too!

The entire family was now saved. What a joy it was when all of us went to church together and wanted to!

CONCLUSION

Now here is the reason I wanted this testimony published. My wife and I have told the story at a lot of churches, and sometimes a person will come forward who hasn't already been saved. But not very many. I want this story to reach people who don't go to church, who think it's all baloney, just like I did. I was wrong. I don't want anyone to go to hell. You can throw this little book across the room if you want, but go pick it up again and give it another shot.

After all my Grandmother's prayers, I was such a hard-head that God had to allow me to die before I found out that He loved me, and that He listens to old ladies who sit in rocking chairs and talk to Him every night. I pray there is someone in your family, or even a close friend, who will never stop mentioning you to God.

INVITATION TO CHRIST

If you have never formerly accepted Christ as your personal Lord and Savior, Scripture says in *Romans 10: 9-13 (NIV)*, *"If you declare with your mouth, 'Jesus is Lord,' and believe in your heart that God raised him from the dead, you will be saved. For it is with your heart that you believe and are justified, and it is with your mouth that you profess your faith and are saved. As Scripture says, 'Anyone who believes in him will never be put to shame.' For there is no difference between Jew and Gentile – the same Lord is Lord of all and richly blesses all who call on him for, 'Everyone who calls on the name of the Lord will be saved.'"*

When you call upon the Lord and invite Him into your life as your Lord and Savior, all your past, present and future sins are forgiven, and your soul will go to Heaven to live with God for eternity.

Do you want to be sure you will go to Heaven?

Say the prayer below out loud, in faith and after you do, tell a trusted Christian friend, pray, get baptized, find a good Bible believing church and -- welcome to the family of God! You are now His beloved son or daughter!

The Salvation Prayer:

(Say this prayer ALOUD. . .)

Lord Jesus, I believe that You came to this Earth and died for my sins on the cross at Calvary. I believe that you sacrificed Your life for me on the cross, so that I may live.

I believe that you were buried and rose from the dead and that now You are alive, seated at the right hand of God the Father in Heaven. I believe that the cross has made a way for me to be fully forgiven and that you are the "door" to enter into Heaven.

I confess that I am a sinner, and I repent of all my sins. I believe and accept Your forgiveness. "Create in me a pure heart, O God, and renew a steadfast spirit within me." (Psalm 51:10 NIV)

I now ask that You to come into my heart and be my Lord and Savior for eternity. Come and fill me with Your Holy Spirit.

Help me to trust in You, to love others and follow You all the days of my life!

I thank you for all that you have done in my life.

It's a New Beginning for you; you are now born again.

AILEEN McNAMARA'S TESTIMONY

Aileen remembers well that fateful late afternoon when Robert did not come home after jogging. Her son was sitting on the steps. She asked him, "Where is your dad?" With a worried look, their young son, Shannon, replied that he didn't know. At that point, both Aileen and her son went looking for Robert at the beach. The book goes into detail of her search, but what the book does not reveal is what Aileen speaks of now.

Upon entering the hospital room, she found Robert strapped to his gurney. The paramedics and doctors told her that they kept him that way because upon pulling him out of the ambulance and transferring him to a gurney, he grabbed the male nurse's arms and threw him across the room. He was murmuring and screaming for God to help him. They did not know if he would continue to be combative and for this reason, he remained strapped down at his arms and legs.

After recovering, the next day, Robert asked for a Bible. Aileen was shocked. He had been a book buyer and gave Bibles away because he never wanted to read one. And now, even though his vision was blurred, he requested a Bible just to have it next to him on his nightstand. Robert often fell asleep with his hand on the Bible as well, as he would lay it in his lap.

He told Aileen that he had gone to hell. He also told Aileen that he learned three things: There is a God, there is a Heaven and there certainly was a hell. He told her that there were demons dragging him and that he had no free choice any longer. He had to go where they put him. He said they would torture and mock him.

He also remembered hearing people, and in the distance, seeing a huge chasm, with flames bursting through. The horror was unbelievable, as he was still alive, but had absolutely no freedom of choice whatsoever.

He cried out to God, and he found himself back in his body. He was afraid and sobbing. From this point on, he had peace and a concrete knowing that God is real. He also knew came to know that God's Word is Truth and that after you die, you go to either of these two places.

Also, his memories of hell had been so horrific in the hospital that the crying, and the screaming, lasted several days off and on. Eventually, Robert found peace, and Aileen states that the Lord healed his memory, so that quite frankly, he "would not be a basket case anymore."

ABOUT THE AUTHOR

Robert McNamara was born in the 1930's. He was an aspiring actor, playwright and author. He appeared in several movies and also played the bailiff in the 1980's comedy television series "Night Court." He was married to Aileen, and together, they have three children, now grown adults with their own children.

Robert wrote, *Snatched From Hell: So Little is Known*, before his death in 2016. This book has been published to let others know of his real-life death experience and his visit to a place called hell. After this traumatic experience, Robert lived a full, vibrant life and became a devoted Christian man.

Made in United States
Orlando, FL
09 April 2023